Inglés sin Barreras®

El Video-Maestro de Inglés Conversacional

2 Conociéndonos más

Cuaderno de ejercicios

Para información sobre
Inglés sin Barreras
en oferta especial de
Referido Preferido
1-800-305-6472
Dé el Código 03429

ISBN: 1-59172-304-3   I704WB02

Conociéndonos más

Índice

No se olvide de estudiar las lecciones en el manual antes de hacer los ejercicios de este cuaderno.

Examen inicial

Antes de comenzar el estudio de este volumen, dedique unos minutos a contestar a las 15 preguntas del examen siguiente. Llene el círculo correspondiente a la respuesta correcta.

1. The children _____ blond hair.
   - ○ a) has
   - ○ b) have
   - ○ c) are
   - ○ d) doesn't have
   - ○ e) are not

2. He _____ tall. He's short.
   - ○ a) have
   - ○ b) does
   - ○ c) has
   - ○ d) isn't
   - ○ e) hasn't

3. Are you hungry? No, _____.
   - ○ a) I'm not
   - ○ b) you aren't
   - ○ c) she isn't
   - ○ d) not hungry
   - ○ e) not

4. _____ you tired?
   - ○ a) They are
   - ○ b) Is
   - ○ c) Are
   - ○ d) Isn't
   - ○ e) Do

5. We _____ angry.
   - ○ a) don't
   - ○ b) isn't
   - ○ c) is
   - ○ d) doesn't
   - ○ e) feel

6. _____ they feel happy or sad?
   - ○ a) Is
   - ○ b) Aren't
   - ○ c) Do
   - ○ d) Who
   - ○ e) What

7. That_____ has long red hair.
   - ○ a) people
   - ○ b) men
   - ○ c) woman
   - ○ d) women
   - ○ e) girls

8. Does he have _____ hair?
   - ○ a) red or red
   - ○ b) short or tall
   - ○ c) green or brown
   - ○ d) curly or straight
   - ○ e) sad or happy

9. _____ the boys feel?
   - ○ a) How
   - ○ b) Do
   - ○ c) How do
   - ○ d) Short
   - ○ e) Do short

10. He is very _____.
    - ○ a) infant
    - ○ b) pretty
    - ○ c) beautiful
    - ○ d) middle-aged
    - ○ e) handsome

11. We are a little _____
    - ○ a) thirsty
    - ○ b) blue eyes
    - ○ c) red hair
    - ○ d) students
    - ○ e) not hungry

12. _____ No, he's excited.
    - ○ a) Does he have short hair?
    - ○ b) Are they tired?
    - ○ c) Is she hungry?
    - ○ d) Is he tall or short?
    - ○ e) Is he bored?

13. I'm not a child! I'm a _____.
    - ○ a) baby
    - ○ b) teenager
    - ○ c) Martin
    - ○ d) infant
    - ○ e) Nancy

14. Does the man have blue or green eyes? _____
    - ○ a) Yes, he has eyes.
    - ○ b) He doesn't have hair.
    - ○ c) No, he doesn't.
    - ○ d) Yes, he green or blue eyes.
    - ○ e) He has green eyes.

15. Is the teacher single _____
    - ○ a) or married.
    - ○ b) and married.
    - ○ c) and not married.
    - ○ d) and married?
    - ○ e) or married?

Cuando haya estudiado todas las lecciones de este volumen, haga el mismo examen de nuevo. Lo encontrará al final de este cuaderno, en la página titulada "Examen final".

Compare los resultados obtenidos en este examen con los del examen final. Así comprobará lo que ha aprendido y podrá medir su progreso.

Cuando haya terminado este examen, empiece a estudiar la Lección uno.

Lección

Encontrará las respuestas en la página 12.

**A. Escriba oraciones que describan estos dibujos.
Use las palabras entre paréntesis.**

Ejemplo: (young) ____*He is young.*____

1. (tall) _____

2. (short) _____

3. (pretty) _____

4. (thin) _____

5. (fat) _____

Encontrará las respuestas en la página 12.

6. (old) _____

7. (handsome) _____

8. (ugly) _____

B. Escriba oraciones que describan estos dibujos. Use las palabras entre paréntesis.

Ejemplo: (blue) _He has blue eyes._

1. (green) _____

2. (brown)_____

Encontrará las respuestas en la página 12.

3. (red) _____

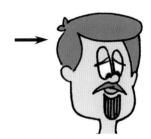

4. (brown)_____

5. (black) _____

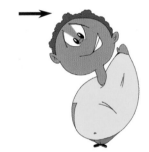

6. (curly) _____

7. (long) _____

8. (bald) _____

Clase

Encontrará las respuestas en la página 12.

C. Debajo de cada oración, escriba otra que tenga el significado contrario.

Ejemplo: He is fat.

*He is thin.*_____

1. I have curly hair.

   _____

2. They are pretty.

   _____

3   She has short hair.

   _____

4. He is ugly.

   _____

5. We are old.

   _____

6. I am fat.

   _____

7. They are tall.

   _____

Encontrará las respuestas en la página 12.

Kathy and Robert

Dan

Kathy

Janet

Bill

Amy, Ann and Dan

D. Complete las oraciones usando los nombres de los personajes que aparecen en las fotografías.

1. _____ has short, curly hair.

2. _____ have long, straight hair.

3. _____ is young. She has blue eyes.

4. _____ are thin.

5. _____ are middle-aged.

6. _____ has short, black hair. He has brown eyes.

Encontrará las respuestas en la página 13.

Complete el diálogo.

Maribel y Margarita están hablando del sobrino y de la sobrina de Margarita.

Margarita   Hi, _____.

Maribel   Hi. How _____ you?

Margarita   I _____ fine. Look.

Maribel   Oh, she _____ cute.

Margarita   Thank you.

Maribel   _____ she your daughter?

Margarita   No, she _____. She's my niece.

Maribel   Who _____ he?

Margarita   This is _____ nephew.

Maribel   _____ is nice-looking, too.

Margarita   They _____ curly hair.

Maribel   Do they _____ brown eyes?

Margarita   No, _____ have blond hair and blue _____.

Maribel   My daughter has blond hair and _____ eyes, too.

Encontrará las respuestas en la página 13.

Complete las oraciones. Cada una de las oraciones debe describir el dibujo correspondiente.

(b) 1. _____ tall and thin. (d) 5. _____ curly hair.

(b) 2. _____ gray hair. (e) 6. _____ short hair.

(a) 3. _____ brown hair. (c) 7. _____ middle-aged.

(d) 4. _____ young. (f) 8. _____ bald.

Vocabulario

A.
1. She is tall.
2. He is short.
3. She is pretty.
4. He is thin.
5. He is fat.
6. She is old.
7. He is handsome.
8. She is ugly.

B.
1. She has green eyes.
2. She has brown eyes.
3. She has red hair.
4. He has brown hair.
5. He has black hair.
6. He has curly hair.
7. She has long hair.
8. He is bald.

Clase

C.
1. I have straight hair.
2. They are ugly.
3. She has long hair.
4. He is handsome.
5. We are young.
6. I am thin.
7. They are short.

D.
1. Dan
2. Janet and Kathy
3. Kathy
4. Kathy and Robert
5. Amy, Ann and Dan
6. Bill

Diálogo

Margarita	Hi, <u>Maribel</u>.
Maribel	Hi. How <u>are</u> you?
Margarita	I <u>am</u> fine. Look.
Maribel	Oh, she <u>is</u> cute.
Margarita	Thank you.
Maribel	<u>Is</u> she your daughter?
Margarita	No, she <u>isn't</u>. She's my niece.
Maribel	Who <u>is</u> he?
Margarita	This is <u>my</u> nephew.
Maribel	<u>He</u> is nice-looking, too.
Margarita	They <u>have</u> curly hair.
Maribel	Do they <u>have</u> brown eyes?
Margarita	No, <u>they</u> have blond hair and blue <u>eyes</u>.
Maribel	My daughter has blond hair and <u>blue</u> eyes, too.

Examen

1. She is
2. She has
3. They have
4. He is
5. He has
6. They have
7. He is
8. He is

2 Notas

Lección 2

Inglés sin Barreras

Encontrará las respuestas en la página 23.

A. Escriba oraciones negativas partiendo de las oraciones siguientes.

Ejemplo: They are middle-aged.

They aren't middle-aged.

1. I am thin.

   _____

2. We are beautiful.

   _____

3. The boy is sad.

   _____

4. He is handsome.

   _____

5. The girls are cute.

   _____

6. She is average.

   _____

Encontrará las respuestas en la página 23.

B. Escriba las preguntas correspondientes a estas oraciones.

Ejemplo: They are middle-aged.

Are they middle-aged?

1. Miranda is cute.

   _____

2. We are tall.

   _____

3. The people are beautiful.

   _____

4. He is average.

   _____

5. The boys are short.

   _____

6. He is bald.

   _____

Encontrará las respuestas en la página 23.

C. Conteste a las preguntas relacionadas con los dibujos. Escriba respuestas completas siguiendo el ejemplo indicado a continuación.

Ejemplo: Is she old?

No, she isn't. She's young.

1. Is she ugly?

2. Is he ugly?

3. Is she thin?

4. Are they old?

Encontrará las respuestas en la página 23.

5. Is the woman short?

_____

6. Are they beautiful?

_____

D. Ponga las letras de cada palabra en el orden correcto. Formará palabras del vocabulario de esta lección.

Ejemplo: aft _____ *fat* _____

1. eeoplp _____ *p* _____

2. gyuno _____ *y* _____

3. nashdoem _____ *h* _____

4. nowma _____ *w* _____

5. ddemil-gead _____ *m* _____

6. uutebflai _____ *b* _____

7. gaareve _____ *a* _____

8. thsairgt _____ *s* _____

Encontrará las respuestas en la página 24.

Complete el diálogo.

Tony llama a casa de Ana. Quiere hablar con la madre de Ana.
Ana contesta el teléfono.

Ana   Hello.

Tony   Hi. _____ Joanne there?

Ana   No. _____ 's calling?

Tony   _____ name is Tony. Who are _____ ?

Ana   I'm _____ daughter, Ana.

Tony   Oh. _____ very tall, aren't you?

Ana   No. I'm _____ .

Tony   You have blond _____ .

Ana   No, I _____ brown hair.

Tony   Are your _____ green?

Ana   No, _____ blue. My mother _____ green eyes.

       Are you _____ or short?

Tony   Hmmm…I'm average.

Ana   _____ you thin or fat?

Tony   _____ average!

Ana   Are _____ handsome or ugly?

Tony   I'm handsome!

Encontrará las respuestas en la página 24.

Escriba las preguntas correspondientes a estas oraciones usando las palabras entre paréntesis.

Ejemplo: *Am I short?*
No, you aren't. You are tall.

1. _____
   No, they aren't. They are very handsome.

2. _____
   No, he isn't. He's a little fat.

3. (you)_____
   No, we aren't. We're young.

4. (you)_____
   No, I'm not. I'm short.

5. _____
   No, she isn't. She's very pretty.

6. (you) _____
   No, I'm not. I'm middle-aged.

Vocabulario

A.
1. I'm not thin.
2. We aren't beautiful.
3. The boy isn't sad.
4. He isn't handsome.
5. The girls aren't cute.
6. She isn't average.

B.
1. Is Miranda cute?
2. Are we tall?
3. Are the people beautiful?
4. Is he average?
5. Are the boys short?
6. Is he bald?

Clase

C.
1. No, she isn't. She's pretty (*or* beautiful).
2. No, he isn't. He's handsome.
3. No, she isn't. She's fat.
4. No, they aren't. They're young.
5. No, she isn't. She's tall.
6. No, they aren't. They're ugly.

D.
1. people
2. young
3. handsome
4. woman
5. middle-aged
6. beautiful
7. average
8. straight

Diálogo

Ana   Hello.

Tony   Hi. <u>Is</u> Joanne there?

Ana   No. <u>Who</u>'s calling?

Tony   <u>My</u> name is Tony. Who are <u>you</u>?

Ana   I'm <u>her</u> (*or* Joanne's) daughter, Ana.

Tony   Oh. <u>You're</u> very tall, aren't you?

Ana   No. I'm <u>short</u> (*or* not).

Tony   You have blond <u>hair</u>.

Ana   No, I <u>have</u> brown hair.

Tony   Are your <u>eyes</u> green?

Ana   No, <u>they're</u> blue. My mother <u>has</u> green eyes. Are you <u>tall</u> or short?

Tony   Hmmm…I'm average.

Ana   <u>Are</u> you thin or fat?

Tony   <u>I'm</u> average!

Ana   Are <u>you</u> handsome or ugly?

Tony   I'm handsome!

Examen

1. Are they ugly?
2. Is he thin?
3. Are you old?
4. Are you tall?
5. Is she ugly?
6. Are you young? *or* Are you old?

Lección

Encontrará las respuestas en la página 36.

A. Escriba oraciones que describan estos dibujos.

Ejemplo: _They are happy._

1. _____

2. _____

3. _____

4. _____

5. _____

Encontrará las respuestas en la página 36.

6.

7.

8. _____

9. _____

10. _____

Encontrará las respuestas en la página 36.

B. Sopa de letras

Encuentre las palabras de la lista siguiente en el cuadro de abajo.
Las palabras se leen de izquierda a derecha y de arriba abajo.

angry, cold, crazy, happy, hot, hungry, nervous,
sad, scared, sick, sleepy, thirsty, tired

X	C	S	I	C	K	H	T
H	O	T	S	I	A	U	H
Y	L	Y	L	P	N	N	I
B	D	S	E	M	G	G	R
T	D	C	E	O	R	R	S
I	H	A	P	P	Y	Y	T
R	F	R	Y	S	A	D	Y
E	N	E	R	V	O	U	S
D	G	D	C	R	A	Z	Y

Encontrará las respuestas en la página 36.

C. Convierta estas oraciones en oraciones negativas y en plural.

Ejemplo: The boy is happy.   *The boys aren't happy.*

1.   The teacher is hot.

   _____

2.   The student is hungry.

   _____

3.   The woman is scared.

   _____

4.   The man is handsome.

   _____

5.   The child is young.

   _____

6.   The person is sleepy.

   _____

Encontrará las respuestas en la página 37.

D. Dibuje una línea que una cada dibujo con el dibujo de significado contrario.

poor

single

hot

excited

happy

mean

sad

nice

rich

bored

married

cold

Encontrará las respuestas en la página 37.

E. Ahora que ya tiene formadas las parejas de dibujos, escriba preguntas usando las palabras entre paréntesis y la palabra "or."

Ejemplo (he, rich) _Is he rich or poor?_

1. (she, single) _____

2. (you, hot) _____

3. (they, excited) _____

4. (you, happy) _____

5. (he, mean) _____

Encontrará las respuestas en la página 37.

Ponga las oraciones de este diálogo en el orden correcto.

Paula está hablando con su padre. Paula no se encuentra bien.

_____ I feel a little tired.

___*1*___ Hi, Paula.

_____ Yes, you are hot.

_____ How are you?

_____ Tired? Are you thirsty, too?

_____ No, I'm not hungry. I feel hot.

_____ Good evening, Dad.

_____ Yes, I am very thirsty.

_____ Are you hungry?

Encontrará las respuestas en la página 37.

Conteste a las preguntas relacionadas con los dibujos siguiendo el ejemplo indicado a continuación.

Ejemplo: Are they excited?

No, they aren't. They're bored.

1.   Is she sleepy?

_____

2.   Is she hot?

_____

3.   Are they thirsty?

_____

4.   Is she angry?

_____

Encontrará las respuestas en la página 37.

5. Are they happy?

_____

6. Is he angry?

_____

7. Is she young or old?

_____

8. Is she thirsty or sick?

_____

Vocabulario

A.
1. She is hot.
2. She is scared.
3. She is thirsty.
4. They are angry.
5. She is sleepy (*or* tired).
6. She is sick.
7. She is sad.
8. They are hungry.
9. She is cold.
10. She is nervous

B.

X	C	S	I	C	K	H	T
H	O	T	S	I	A	U	H
Y	L	Y	L	P	N	N	I
B	D	S	E	M	G	G	R
T	D	C	E	O	R	R	S
I	H	A	P	P	Y	Y	T
R	F	R	Y	S	A	D	Y
E	N	E	R	V	O	U	S
D	G	D	C	R	A	Z	Y

Clase

C.
1. The teachers aren't hot.
2. The students aren't hungry.
3. The women aren't scared.
4. The men aren't handsome.
5. The children aren't young.
6. The people aren't sleepy.

D. poor — rich
single — married
hot — cold
excited — bored
happy — sad
mean — nice

E.
1. Is she single or married?
2. Are you hot or cold?
3. Are they excited or bored?
4. Are you happy or sad?
5. Is he mean or nice?

Diálogo

<u>4</u> I feel a little tired.
<u>1</u> Hi, Paula.
<u>9</u> Yes, you are hot.
<u>3</u> How are you?
<u>5</u> Tired? Are you thirsty, too?
<u>8</u> No, I'm not hungry. I feel hot.
<u>2</u> Good evening, Dad.
<u>6</u> Yes, I am very thirsty.
<u>7</u> Are you hungry?

Examen

1. Yes, she is.
2. No, she isn't. She's cold.
3. No, they aren't. They're hungry.
4. No, she isn't. She's scared.
5. Yes, they are.
6. Yes, he is.
7. She's old.
8. She's sick.

4 Notas

Lección

4 Notas

Vocabulario

Encontrará las respuestas en la página 48.

A. Escriba las preguntas correspondientes a estas oraciones siguiendo el ejemplo indicado a continuación.

Ejemplo: They feel scared. *Do they feel scared?*

1. She has red hair. _____

2. They feel angry. _____

3. The boys have blue eyes. _____

4. The girl feels nervous. _____

5. The woman has gray hair. _____

6. The men feel hungry. _____

7. The children have curly hair. _____

8. She feels bored. _____

Encontrará las respuestas en la página 48.

B. Conteste a las preguntas relacionadas con los dibujos usando respuestas cortas.

Ejemplo: Does she feel sick? _Yes, she does._

1. Do they feel thirsty?

_____

2. Does she have gray hair?

_____

3. Does he feel sleepy?

_____

4. Do they feel sad?

_____

Encontrará las respuestas en la página 48.

5. Does he have straight hair?

_____

6. Does the woman feel cold?

_____

7. Do they have black hair?

_____

8. Does the man feel angry?

_____

Encontrará las respuestas en la página 48.

C. Complete las oraciones relacionadas con los dibujos.

Ejemplo: ___*Is*___ the woman scared ___*or*___ angry? She is scared.

1. Walter is _____ tall. _____ is average.

Walter

2. This woman's name is _____ . She has _____ hair.

    She is not short or _____. She is _____ and thin.

Lucy

3. Is Caroline _____ ? No, she isn't. She's a little fat.

Caroline

4. The witches are _____.

5. The baby is not old. He is very _____.

    He feels _____, not sad.

44

Encontrará las respuestas en la página 48.

6. How does the woman _____? She feels _____ .

7. The _____ has _____, blond _____ .

D. Ponga las letras en el orden correcto.

Ejemplo: dsearc *scared* _____

1. ugy   *g* _____

2. vnosreu   *n* _____

3. cyzar   *c* _____

4. ryclu rhia *c* _____

5. eeyspl   *s* _____

6. eesfngli   *f* _____

7. undsett   *s* _____

8. eirtd   *t* _____

Encontrará las respuestas en la página 49.

Complete el diálogo.

Max y Al se saludan cuando está a punto de finalizar el partido de béisbol.
Max está esperando a que su hijo Danny termine el partido.

Al Hi, _____.

Max How's _____ going?

Al I'm OK. How do _____ feel?

Max _____ very tired.

Al Is that your _____?

Max No, my son, Danny, _____ short red hair.

Al _____ that him?

Max No, Danny has blue eyes. And _____'s short.

   There he _____. Hey, Danny!

Danny Hi, Dad.

Max Are you _____?

Danny Yes, I'm a little tired.

Al Hi, Danny. My name's _____ Wilson.

Danny Nice to _____ you, Mr. Wilson.

Al Nice to meet you, too.

Max Let's go home. Bye, Al.

Al See _____ later.

Encontrará las respuestas en la página 49.

Escriba las preguntas correspondientes a estas respuestas.

Ejemplo: _Am I short?_

No, you aren't. You are tall.

1. _____

No, he doesn't. He feels excited.

2. _____

Yes, they are very hungry.

3. _____

No, the woman has blue eyes.

4. _____

Yes, the people feel thirsty.

5. (you) _____

No, I have curly hair.

6. (or) _____

He has straight hair.

Vocabulario

A.
1. Does she have red hair?
2. Do they feel angry?
3. Do the boys have blue eyes?
4. Does the girl feel nervous?
5. Does the woman have gray hair?
6. Do the men feel hungry?
7. Do the children have curly hair?
8. Does she feel bored?

B.
1. No, they don't.
2. Yes, she does.
3. Yes, he does.
4. No, they don't.
5. No, he doesn't.
6. No, she doesn't.
7. No, they don't.
8. Yes, he does.

Clase

C.
1. Walter is <u>not</u> tall. <u>He</u> is average.
2. This woman's name is <u>Lucy</u>. She has <u>gray</u> hair. She is not short or <u>fat</u>. She is <u>tall</u> and thin.
3. Is Caroline <u>thin</u>? No, she isn't. She's a little fat.
4. The witches are <u>ugly</u>.
5. The baby is not old. He is very <u>young</u>. He feels <u>happy</u>, not sad.
6. How does the woman <u>feel</u>? She feels <u>sick</u>.
7. The <u>boy</u> has <u>curly</u> (*or* short) blond <u>hair</u>.

D.
1. guy
2. nervous
3. crazy
4. curly hair
5. sleepy
6. feelings
7. student
8. tired

Diálogo

Al	Hi, <u>Max</u>.
Max	How's <u>it</u> going?
Al	I'm OK. How do <u>you</u> feel?
Max	<u>I'm</u> very tired.
Al	Is that your <u>son</u>?
Max	No, my son, Danny, <u>has</u> short red hair.
Al	<u>Is</u> that him?
Max	No, Danny has blue eyes. And <u>he's</u> short. There he <u>is</u>. Hey, Danny!
Danny	Hi, Dad.
Max	Are you <u>tired</u>?
Danny	Yes, I'm a little tired.
Al	Hi, Danny. My name's <u>Al</u> (or <u>Mr.</u>) Wilson.
Danny	Nice to <u>meet</u> you, Mr. Wilson.
Al	Nice to meet you, too.
Max	Let's go home. Bye, Al.
Al	See <u>you</u> later.

Examen

1. Does he feel bored?
2. Are they hungry?
3. Does the woman have green (*or* brown, *or* gray) eyes?
4. Do the people feel thirsty?
5. Do you have straight hair?
6. Does he have straight hair or curly hair?

V Notas

Aprendamos viajando

Notas

Encontrará las respuestas en la página 55.

Las Vegas

Antes de completar este ejercicio, vea la sección "Aprendamos viajando" incluida en el video y lea la misma sección en el manual.

Si la información contenida en la oración es verdadera, haga un círculo alrededor de la palabra *True*. Si la información es falsa, haga un círculo alrededor de la palabra *False* y escriba una oración con la información correcta.

True *False* 1. Las Vegas is in the state of California.

_____

True *False* 2. Las Vegas is in the middle of a desert.

_____

True *False* 3. Three million people live in Las Vegas.

_____

True *False* 4. The hotels in Las Vegas are very big.

_____

True *False* 5. There are more than 100,000 hotel rooms in the city.

_____

Encontrará las respuestas en la página 55.

True   False   6.   The Golden Nugget has a large diamond.

_____

True   False   7.   There are no bright lights in Las Vegas.

_____

True   False   8. You cannot gamble in a casino.

_____

True   False   9. Las Vegas is a family town.

_____

True   False   10. Hoover Dam is on the California River.

_____

True   False   11. Lake Mead is a two-lane highway.

_____

True   False   12. The Grand Canyon has an airport.

_____

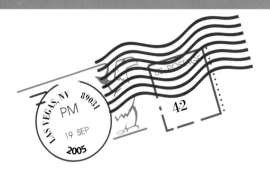

1. False. Las Vegas is in Nevada.
2. True.
3. False. One million people live in Las Vegas.
4. True.
5. True.
6. False. The Golden Nugget has a large gold nugget.
7. False. There are many bright lights.
8. False. You can gamble in a casino.
9. True.
10. False. It's on the Colorado River.
11. False. It's a large lake.
12. True.

Aprendamos conversando

Encontrará las respuestas en la página 64.

Actividad 1. Cómo describir a las personas
Escuche y haga las preguntas.

Is he _____?   Is she _____?

Does he have _____ hair?   Does she have _____ hair?

Is his hair _____?   Is her hair _____?

Does he have _____ eyes?   Does she have _____ eyes?

Are his eyes _____?   Are her eyes _____?

Actividad 2. Los sentimientos
¿Cómo se siente usted? Escuche y repita.

Actividad 3. ¿Cómo se sienten ellos?
Escuche cada sonido y decida cómo se sienten estas personas. Marque con un círculo la respuesta correcta.

1. happy   (sad)

2. happy   sad

3. tired   angry

4. tired   angry

5. hot   scared

6. thirsty   hungry

Encontrará las respuestas en la página 64.

Actividad 4. Opuestos

Escuche y escriba el opuesto de cada palabra.

1. ____ ____ ____ ____ ____
2. ____ ____ ____ ____
3. ____ ____ ____ ____
4. ____ ____ ____
5. ____ ____ ____ ____
6. ____ ____ ____ ____
7. ____ ____ ____ ____
8. ____ ____ ____ ____
9. ____ ____ ____ ____ ____ ____

Escuche y escriba el opuesto de cada palabra.

I'm _____.   I'm not _____.

He's _____.   He isn't_____.

She's_____.   She isn't _____.

Actividad 5. Diálogos

**Escuche los diálogos y escuchará algunas preguntas.
Luego, marque con un círculo la respuesta correcta.**

Diálogo 1. Escuche la conversación entre Janet y Bill.

1. (Yes, it is.)	No, it isn't.	5. Yes, he is.	No, he isn't.
2. Yes, he is.	No, he isn't.	6. Yes, it is.	No, it isn't.
3. Yes, he is.	No, he isn't.	7. Yes, it is.	No, it isn't.
4. Yes, he is.	No, he isn't.	8. Yes, he is.	No, he isn't.

Encontrará las respuestas en la página 64.

Diálogo 2. Ahora escuche la conversación entre Robert y Tom.

1. Yes, he is.   No, it isn't.   4. Yes, he does.   No, he doesn't.

2. Yes, he is.   No, he isn't.   5. Yes, he is.   No, he isn't.

3. Yes, he does.   No, he doesn't.   6. Yes, he is.   No, he isn't.

Diálogo 3. Ahora escuche a Dan y a Kathy.

1. Yes, she is.   No, she isn't.   4. Yes, she does.   No, she doesn't.

2. Yes, she is.   No, she isn't.   5. Yes, she does.   No, she doesn't.

3. Yes, she is.   No, she doesn't.

Diálogo 4. Escuche a Amy y a Bill.

1. Yes, she is.   No, she isn't.   4. Yes, they are.   No, they aren't.

2. Yes, he is.   No, he isn't.   5. Yes, they are.   No, they aren't.

3. Yes, they are.   No, they aren't.

Actividad 6. Pronunciación
Escuche y decida si la persona está diciendo "is" o "isn't", o si dice "are" o "aren't". Marque con un círculo la palabra que oiga.

1. is   isn't   5. are   aren't

2. is   isn't   6. are   aren't

3. are   aren't   7. is   isn't

4. are   aren't   8. is   isn't

Actividad 7. Personas de diferentes edades
Escuche y repita el singular y plural de estas etapas de la vida.

infant - infants   child - children

baby - babies   kid - kids

toddler - toddlers   boy - boys

61

Encontrará las respuestas en la página 65.

girl - girls

teenager - teenagers

adult - adults

man - men

gentleman - gentlemen

guy - guys

woman - women

lady - ladies

gal - gals

senior - seniors

Actividad 8. Pronunciación: la "s" plural

Escuche las palabras siguientes y marque con un círculo el sonido de la "s" plural que usted oiga.

1.	s	(z)	6.	s	z
2.	s	z	7.	s	z
3.	s	z	8.	s	z
4.	s	z	9.	s	z
5.	s	z	10.	s	z

Actividad 9. Pronunciación: Clementine

Escuche y repita cada expresión dos veces. Primero en la manera formal y luego, en la manera informal.

darling

Good morning.

How are you doing?

How is it going?

What's happening?

What's going on?

It was nice talking to you.

He is a nice-looking man.

Encontrará las respuestas en la página 65.

Actividad 10. Formas alternativas
Escuche y repita.

I'm sorry.

I'm so sorry.

I'm really sorry.   Don't worry about it.

I'm very sorry.   It's OK.

I'm terribly sorry.   No problem.

Please forgive me.   It's nothing.

I apologize.   Forget it.

Forget about it.

Actividad 11. Conecciones románticas
Escuche y complete estos mensajes con las palabras
que hacen falta.

Operator: Hello, friends! This is the Free Community Phone Line for

single _____ and _____. To meet a _____, press one.

To meet a _____, press two.

Jeremy: Hi, I'm Jeremy. _____very tall, and I _____ blond

hair and green eyes. _____a very happy guy! _____ you a happy

woman? _____you tall and thin? Then _____ the woman for me!

Oh, I'm really handsome, too. Please leave a message!

Alison: Hello, Jeremy. _____ name is Alison. _____ short

and fat — and a little bald. _____ _____ very happy. But I'm

friendly — and I'm very excited to meet you! Nervous, but excited. Maybe

_____ crazy, but Jeremy, I'm really a very nice person. And maybe a

very good wife for you! Leave a message. Please!

Jeremy: Thanks for _____ message, Alison. This _____ Jeremy.

I'm crazy, too, my darling. I'm _____ _____ and I'm not thin.

I'm really short and fat. And _____ _____ really handsome.

But I think I love you! Please marry me!

Actividad 3.

1. happy   (sad)
2. (happy)   sad
3. (tired)   angry
4. tired   (angry)
5. hot   (scared)
6. (thirsty)   hungry

Actividad 4.

1. S H O R T
2. T H I N
3. U G L Y
4. O L D
5. S H O R T
6. C O L D
7. H A P P Y
8. P O O R
9. S I N G L E

Las respuestas pueden variar.

I'm _____.   I'm not _____.

He's _____.   He isn't_____.

She's_____.   She isn't _____.

Actividad 5.

Diálogo 1.

1. (Yes, it is)   No, it isn't.   5. (Yes, he is)   No, he isn't.
2. Yes, he is.   (No, he isn't)   6. Yes, it is.   (No, it isn't.)
3. Yes, he is.   (No, he isn't)   7. (Yes, it is)   No, it isn't.
4. (Yes, he is)   No, he isn't.   8. (Yes, he is)   No, he isn't.

Diálogo 2.

1. (Yes, he is)   No, it isn't.   4. Yes, he does. (No, he doesn't.)
2. Yes, he is.   (No, he isn't)   5. Yes, he is.   (No, he isn't.)
3. (Yes, he does)   No, he doesn't.   6. (Yes, he is.)   No, he isn't.

Diálogo 3.

1. (Yes, she is)   No, she isn't.   4. (Yes, she does.) No, she doesn't.
2. Yes, she is.   (No, she isn't)   5. Yes, she does. (No, she doesn't.)
3. (Yes, she is)   No, she doesn't.

Diálogo 4.
1. Yes, she is. ⟨No, she isn't⟩ 4.⟨Yes, they are⟩. No, they aren't.
2. Yes, he is. ⟨No, he isn't⟩ 5. Yes, they are. ⟨No, they aren't⟩.
3.⟨Yes, they are⟩. No, they aren't.

Actividad 6.

1.⟨is⟩   isn't   5.⟨are⟩   aren't
2. is   ⟨isn't⟩   6. are   ⟨aren't⟩
3. are   ⟨aren't⟩   7.⟨is⟩   isn't
4.⟨are⟩   aren't   8. is   ⟨isn't⟩

Actividad 8.

1. s   ⟨z⟩   6. s   ⟨z⟩
2. s   ⟨z⟩   7. ⟨s⟩   z
3.⟨s⟩   z   8. s   ⟨z⟩
4. s   ⟨z⟩   9. s   ⟨z⟩
5. s   ⟨z⟩   10. s   ⟨z⟩

Actividad 11.

Operator: Hello, friends! This is the Free Community Phone Line for single _men_ and _women_ . To meet a _man_, press one.
To meet a _woman_, press two.
Jeremy: Hi, I'm Jeremy. _I'm_ very tall, and I _have_ blond hair and green eyes. _I'm_ a very happy guy! _Are_ you a happy woman? _Are_ you tall and thin? Then _you're_ the woman for me! Oh, I'm really handsome, too. Please leave a message!
Alison: Hello, Jeremy. _My_ _name_ is Alison. _I'm_ _short_ and fat — and a little bald. _I'm_ _not_ very happy. But I'm friendly — and I'm very excited to meet you! Nervous, but excited. Maybe _I'm_ crazy, but Jeremy, I'm a very nice person. And maybe a very good wife for you! Leave a message. Please!
Jeremy: Thanks for _your_ message, Alison. This _is_ Jeremy. I'm crazy, too, my darling. I'm _not_ _tall_ and I'm not thin. I'm really short and fat. And _I'm_ _not_ really handsome. But I think I love you! Please marry me!

Notas

Notas

Examen final 2

Llene el círculo correspondiente a la respuesta correcta.

1. The children _____ blond hair.
   - O a) has
   - O b) have
   - O c) are
   - O d) doesn't have
   - O e) are not

2. He _____ tall. He's short.
   - O a) have
   - O b) does
   - O c) has
   - O d) isn't
   - O e) hasn't

3. Are you hungry? No, _____.
   - O a) I'm not
   - O b) you aren't
   - O c) she isn't
   - O d) not hungry
   - O e) not

4. _____ you tired?
   - O a) They are
   - O b) Is
   - O c) Are
   - O d) Isn't
   - O e) Do

5. We _____ angry.
   - O a) don't
   - O b) isn't
   - O c) is
   - O d) doesn't
   - O e) feel

6. _____ they feel happy or sad?
   - O a) Is
   - O b) Aren't
   - O c) Do
   - O d) Who
   - O e) What

7. That_____ has long red hair.
   - O a) people
   - O b) men
   - O c) woman
   - O d) women
   - O e) girls

8. Does he have _____ hair?
   - O a) red or red
   - O b) short or tall
   - O c) green or brown
   - O d) curly or straight
   - O e) sad or happy

9. _____ the boys feel?
   - O a) How
   - O b) Do
   - O c) How do
   - O d) Short
   - O e) Do short

10. He is very _____.
   - O a) infant
   - O b) pretty
   - O c) beautiful
   - O d) middle-aged
   - O e) handsome

11. We are a little _____
   - O a) thirsty
   - O b) blue eyes
   - O c) red hair
   - O d) students
   - O e) not hungry

12. _____ No, he's excited.
   - O a) Does he have short hair?
   - O b) Are they tired?
   - O c) Is she hungry?
   - O d) Is he tall or short?
   - O e) Is he bored?

13. I'm not a child! I'm a _____.
   - O a) baby
   - O b) teenager
   - O c) Martin
   - O d) infant
   - O e) Nancy

14. Does the man have blue or green eyes? _____
   - O a) Yes, he has eyes.
   - O b) He doesn't have hair.
   - O c) No, he doesn't.
   - O d) Yes, he green or blue eyes.
   - O e) He has green eyes.

15. Is the teacher single _____
   - O a) or married.
   - O b) and married.
   - O c) and not married.
   - O d) and married?
   - O e) or married?

Cuando termine el examen, córtelo en la línea de puntos y envíelo a:

Profesores
640 S. San Vicente Boulevard
Los Angeles, California 90048-4618
U.S.A.

Por favor, escriba claramente su nombre y dirección (use tinta oscura) para que podamos enviarle el examen corregido.

Nombre _____

Dirección _____

Ciudad _____ Estado _____

Código Postal _____ País _____

Si prefiere, puede enviarlo por fax al (323) 782-7466.
Responderemos por fax.

Fax(_____) _____

Si desea saber las respuestas de una forma inmediata, visite nuestra página Web, www.isbonline.com, y haga el examen en el Internet.

Si tiene alguna pregunta, envíe un correo electrónico a:
profesores@isbonline.com
Este servicio no está disponible en el estado de California.

Fecha _____

Nº. de contrato _____

Teléfono (_____) _____